KOOKY COLORING BOOK

For All Ages

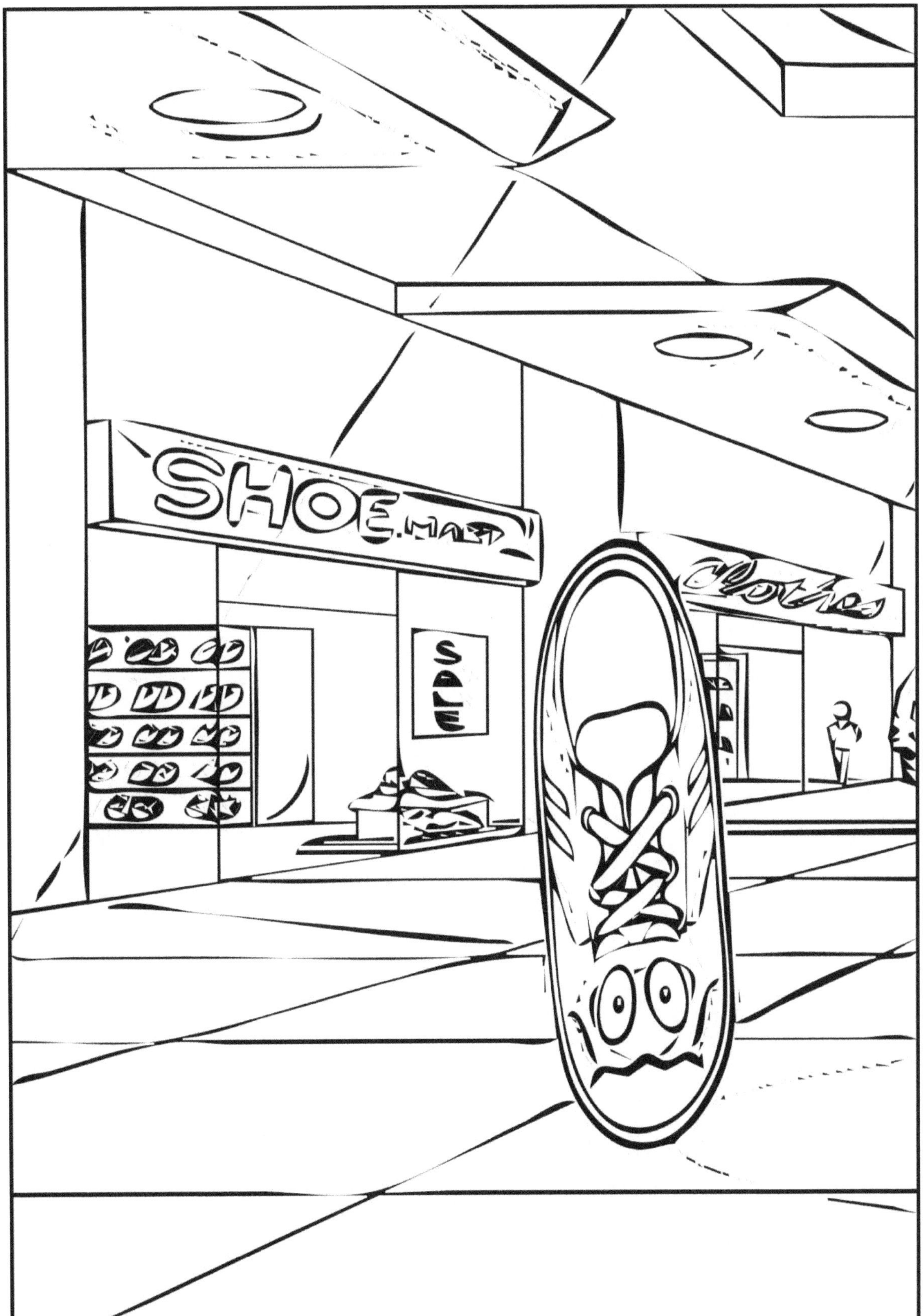
SHOE
SALE
Clothes

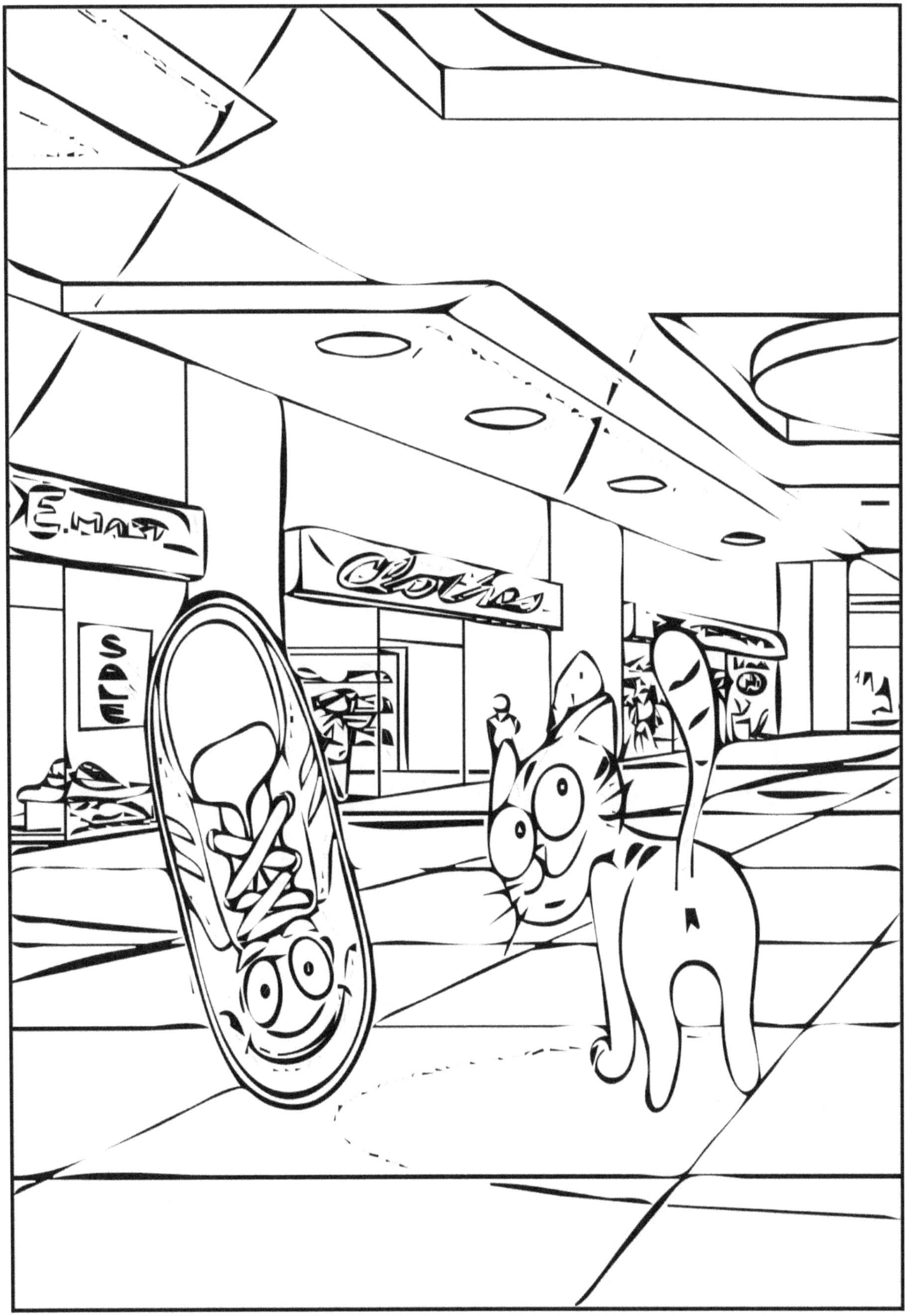
E.MART
Clothes

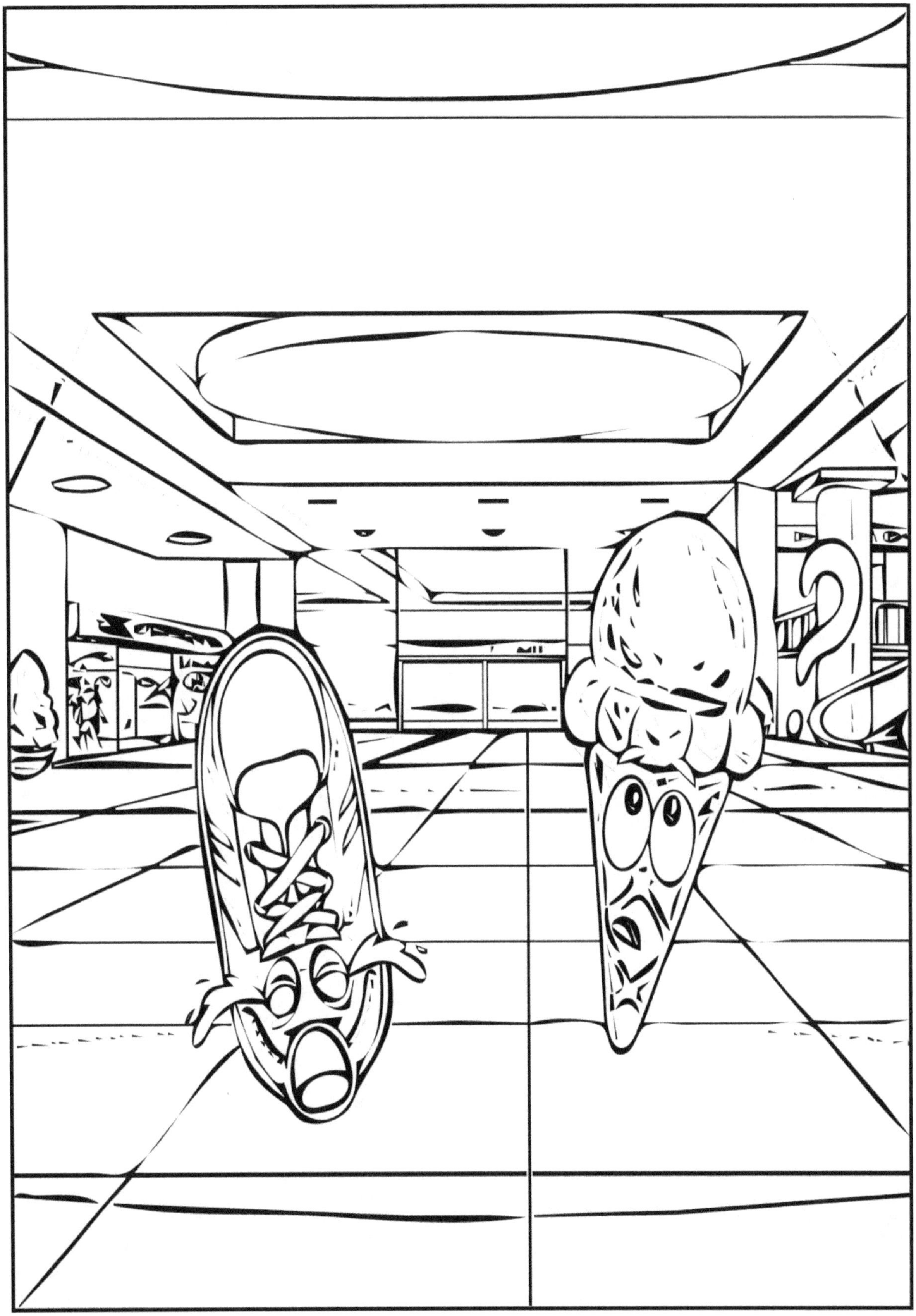

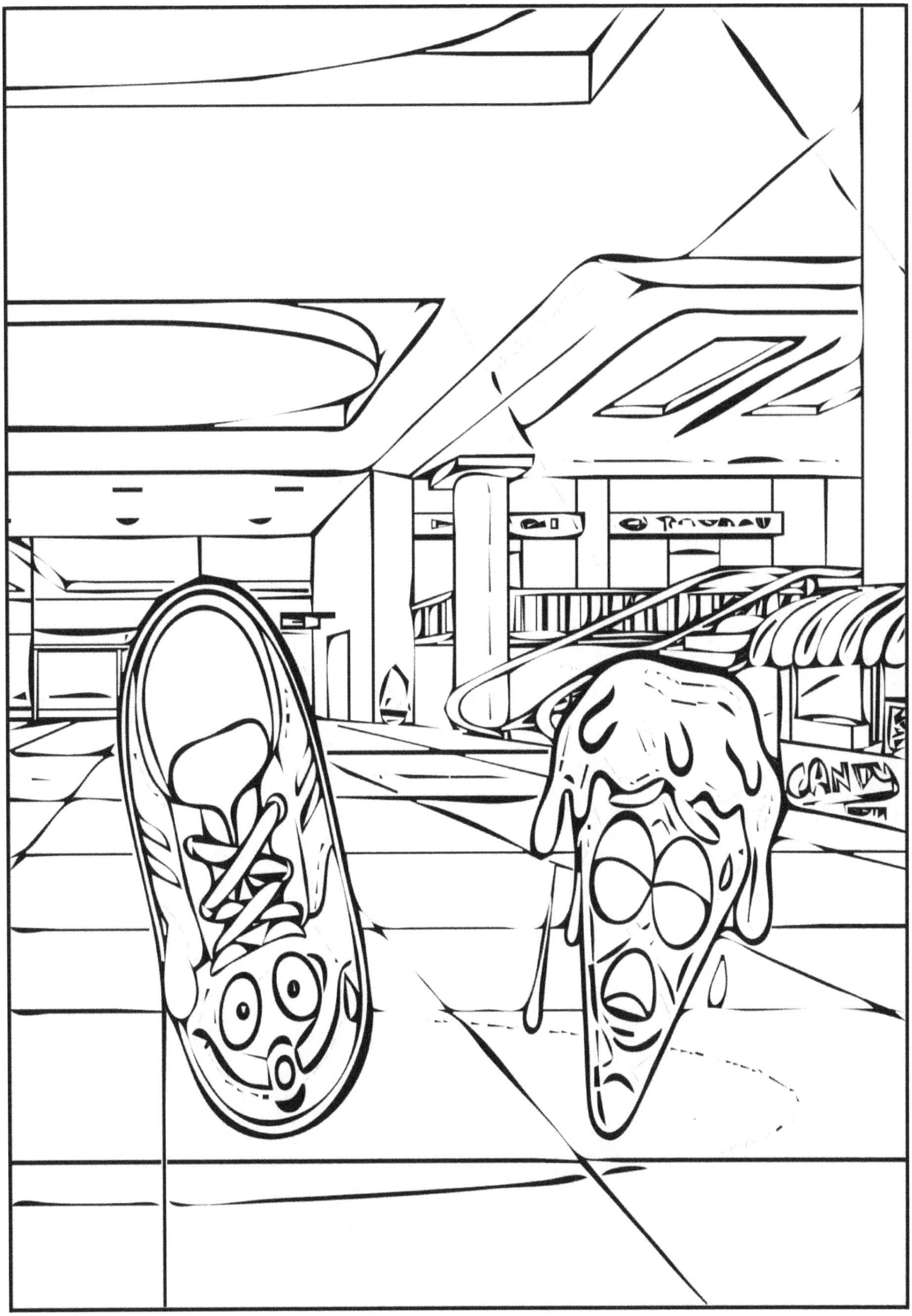
CANDY

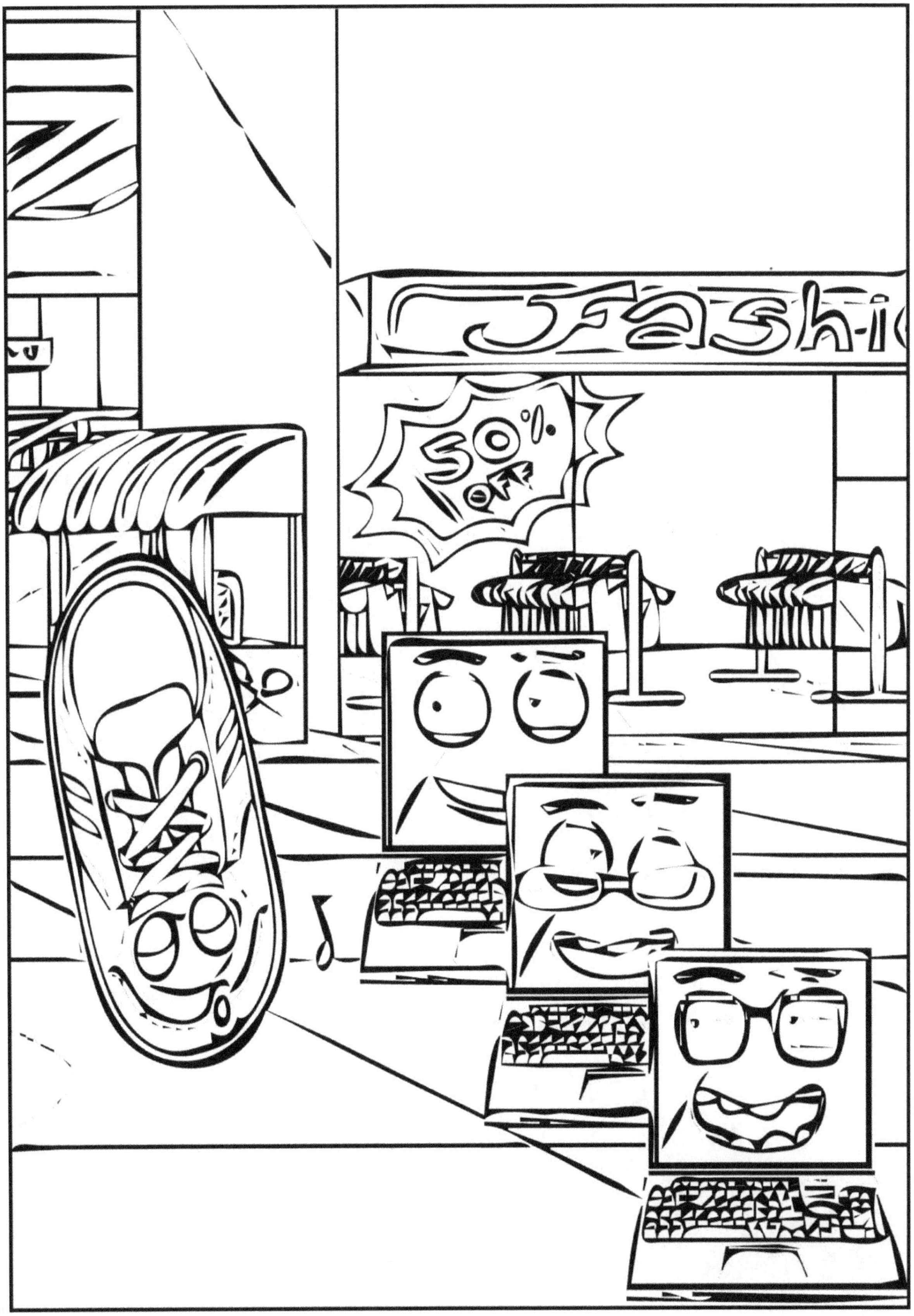
Fashi
50%
OFF

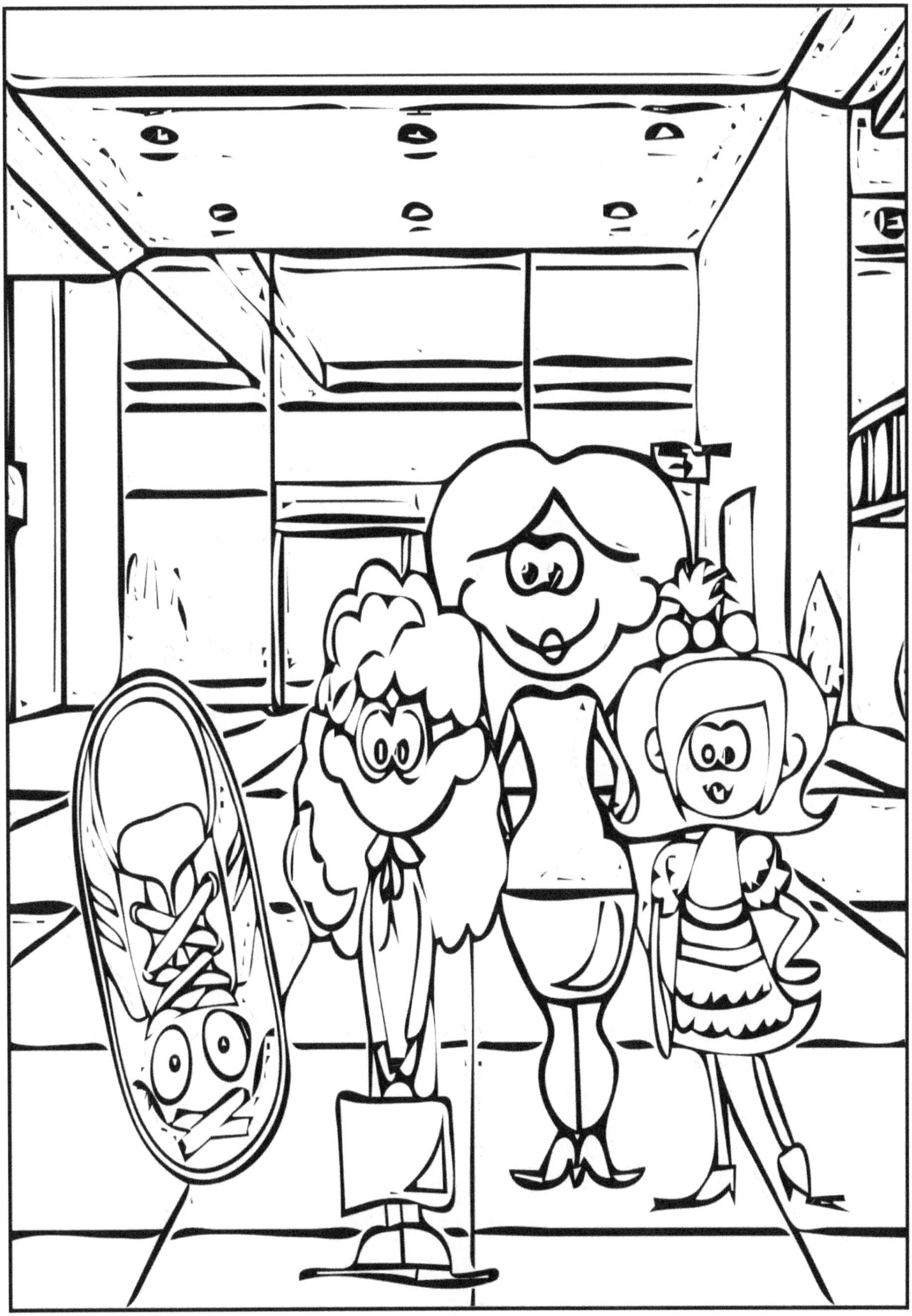

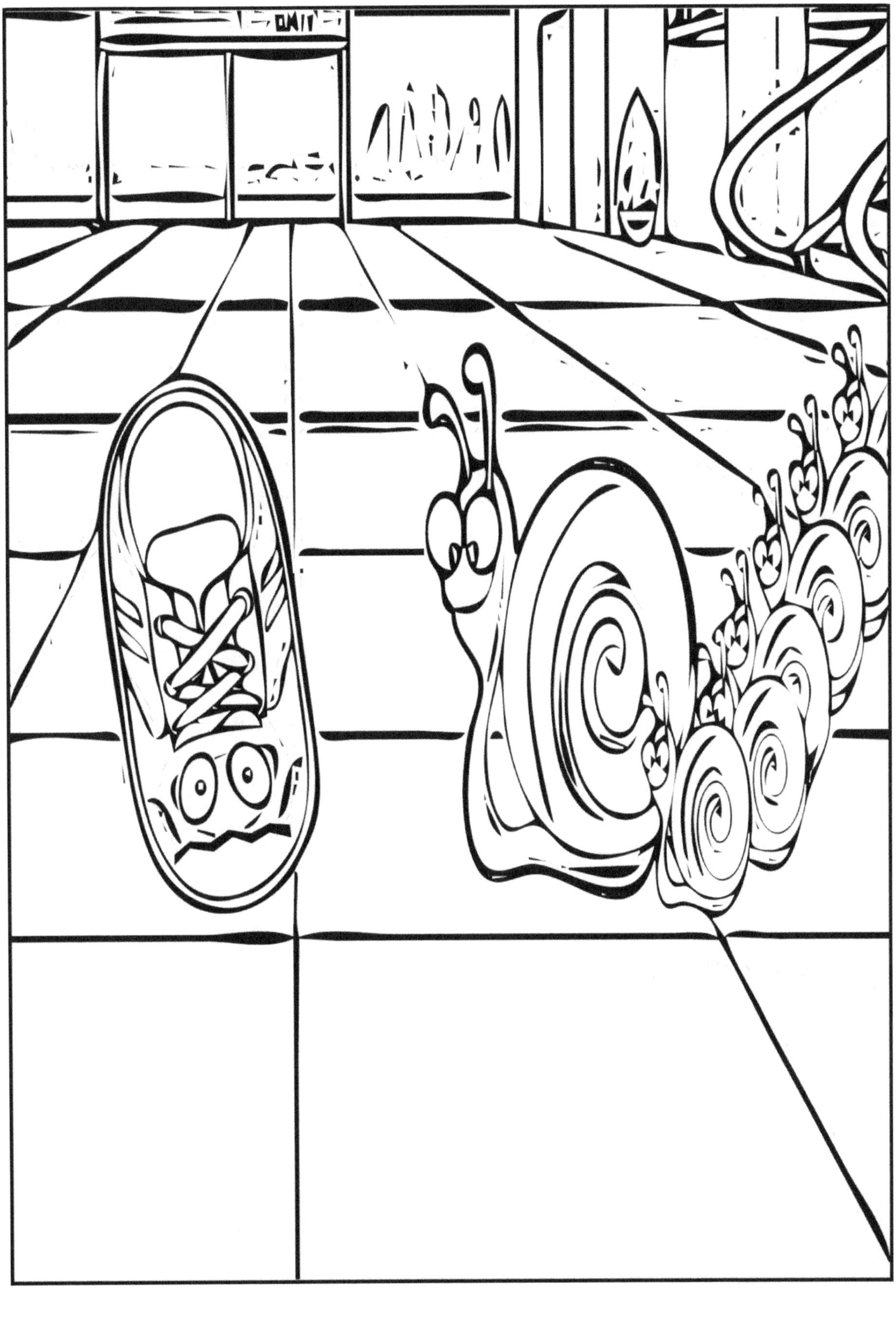

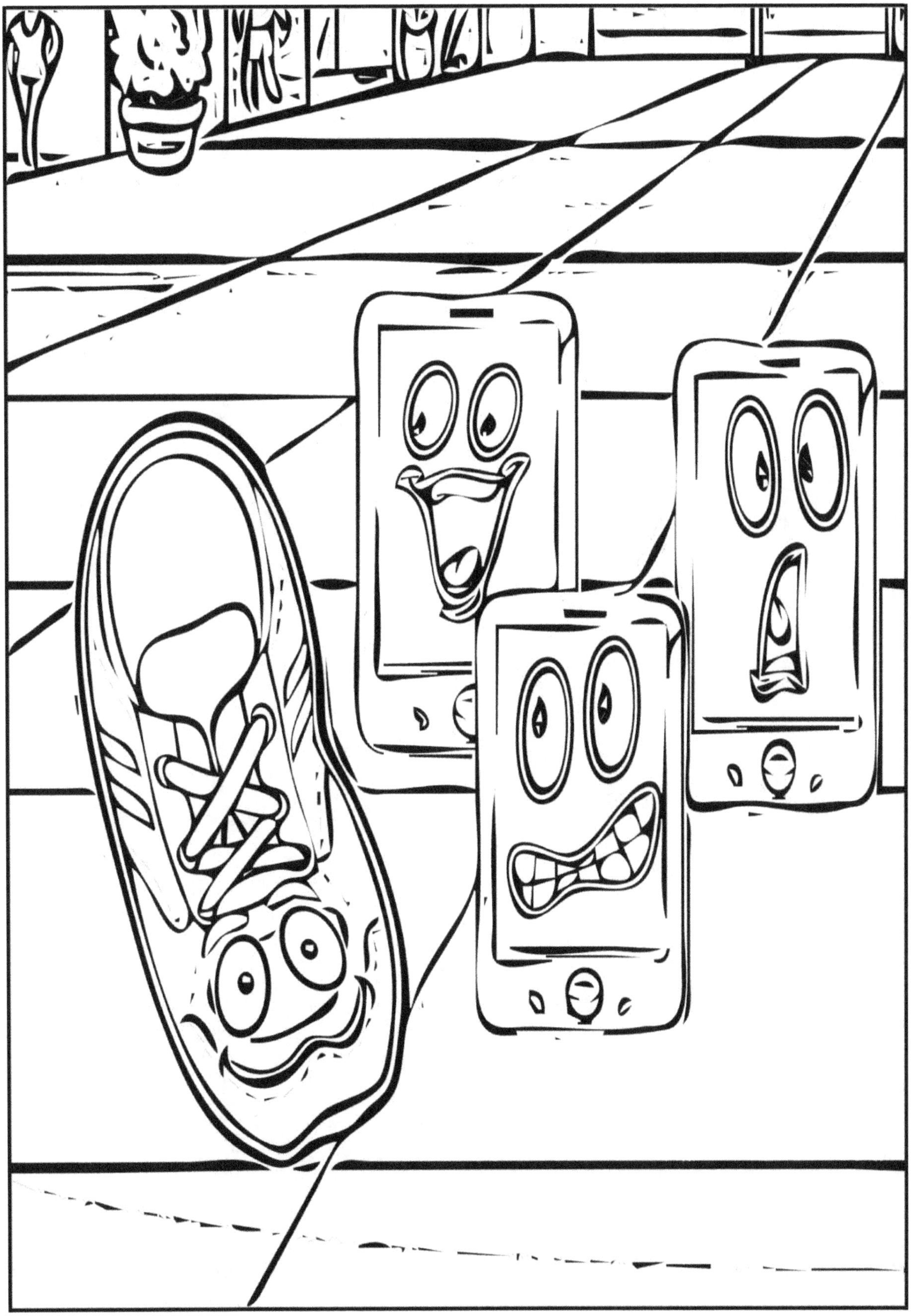

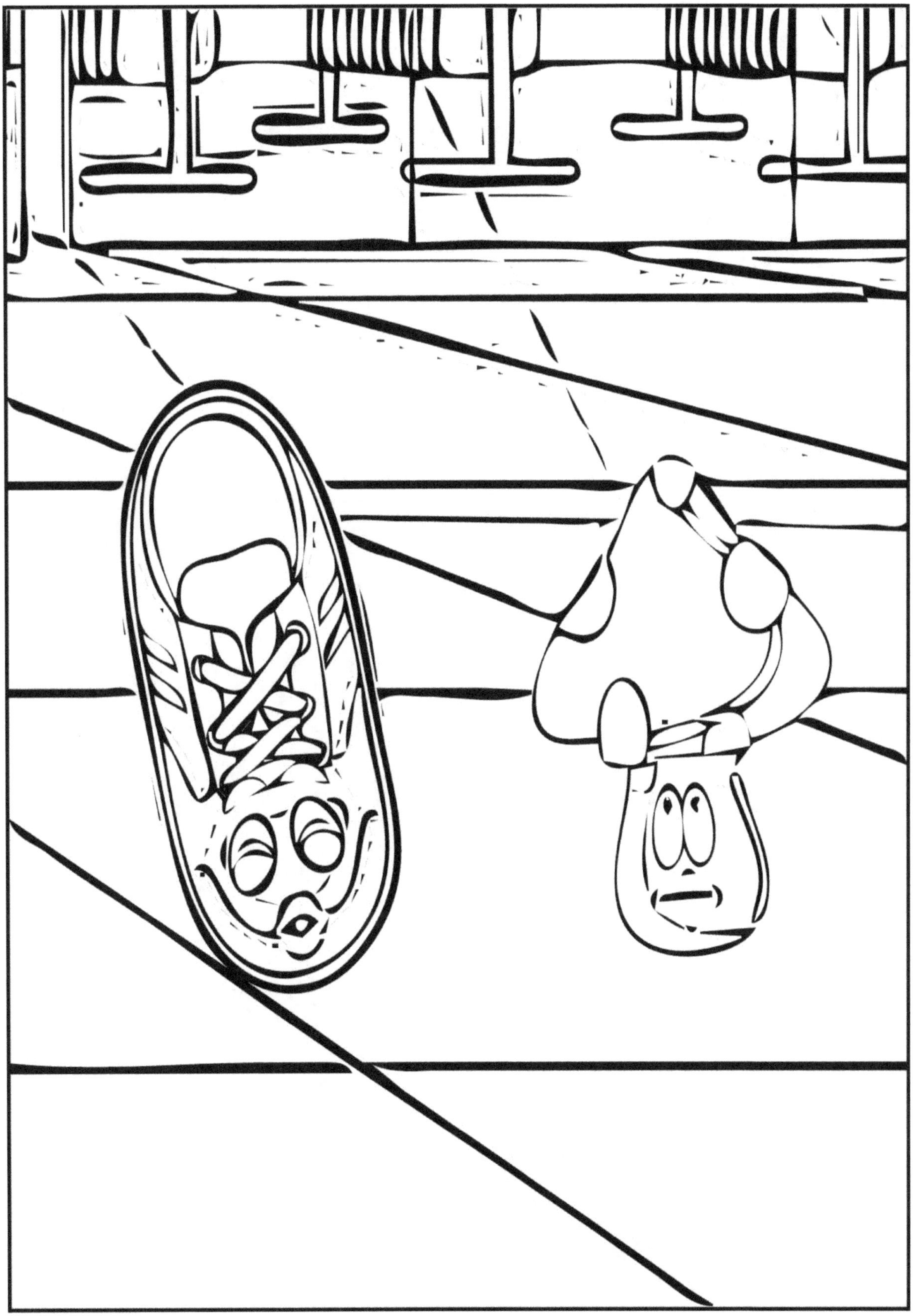

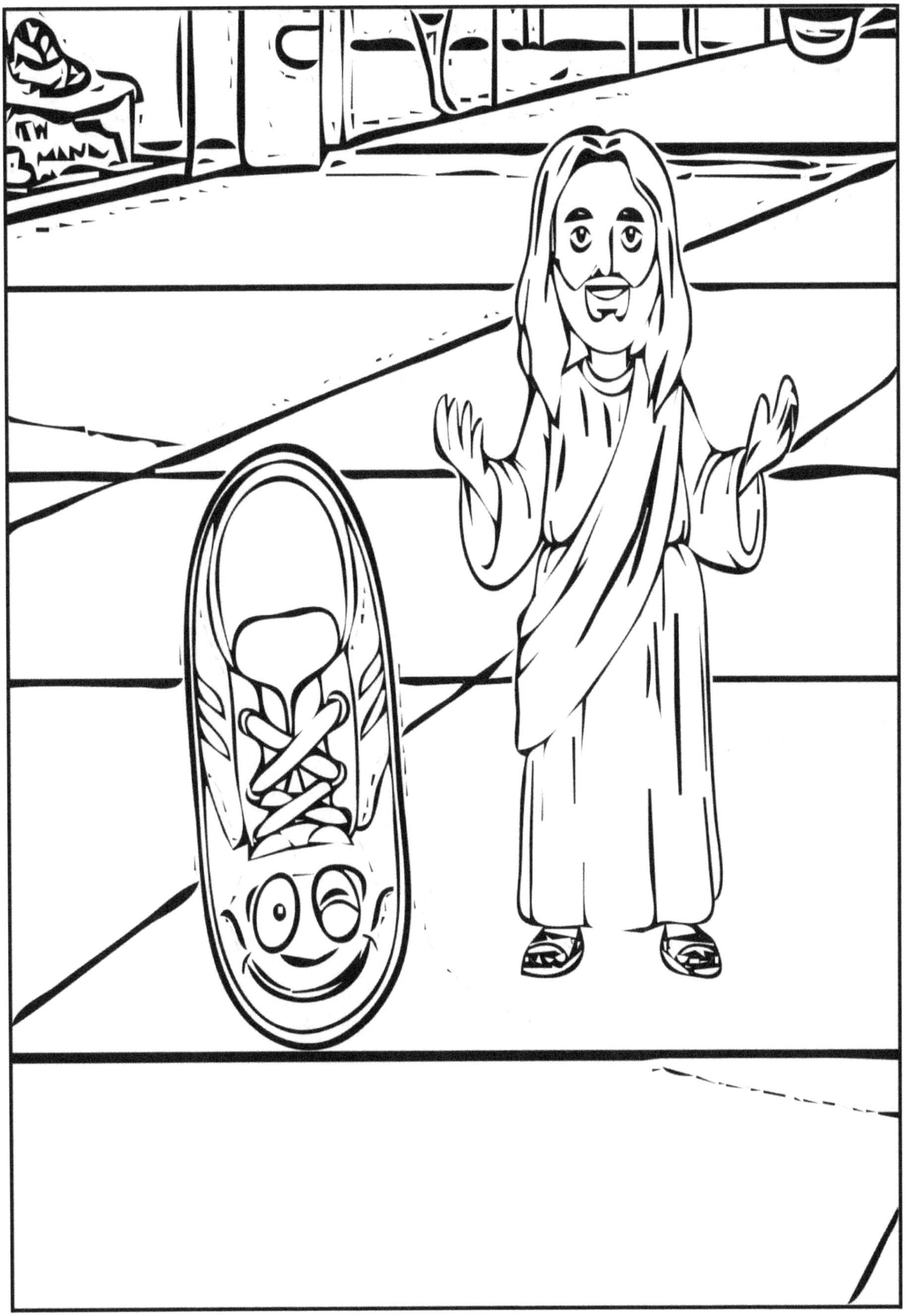

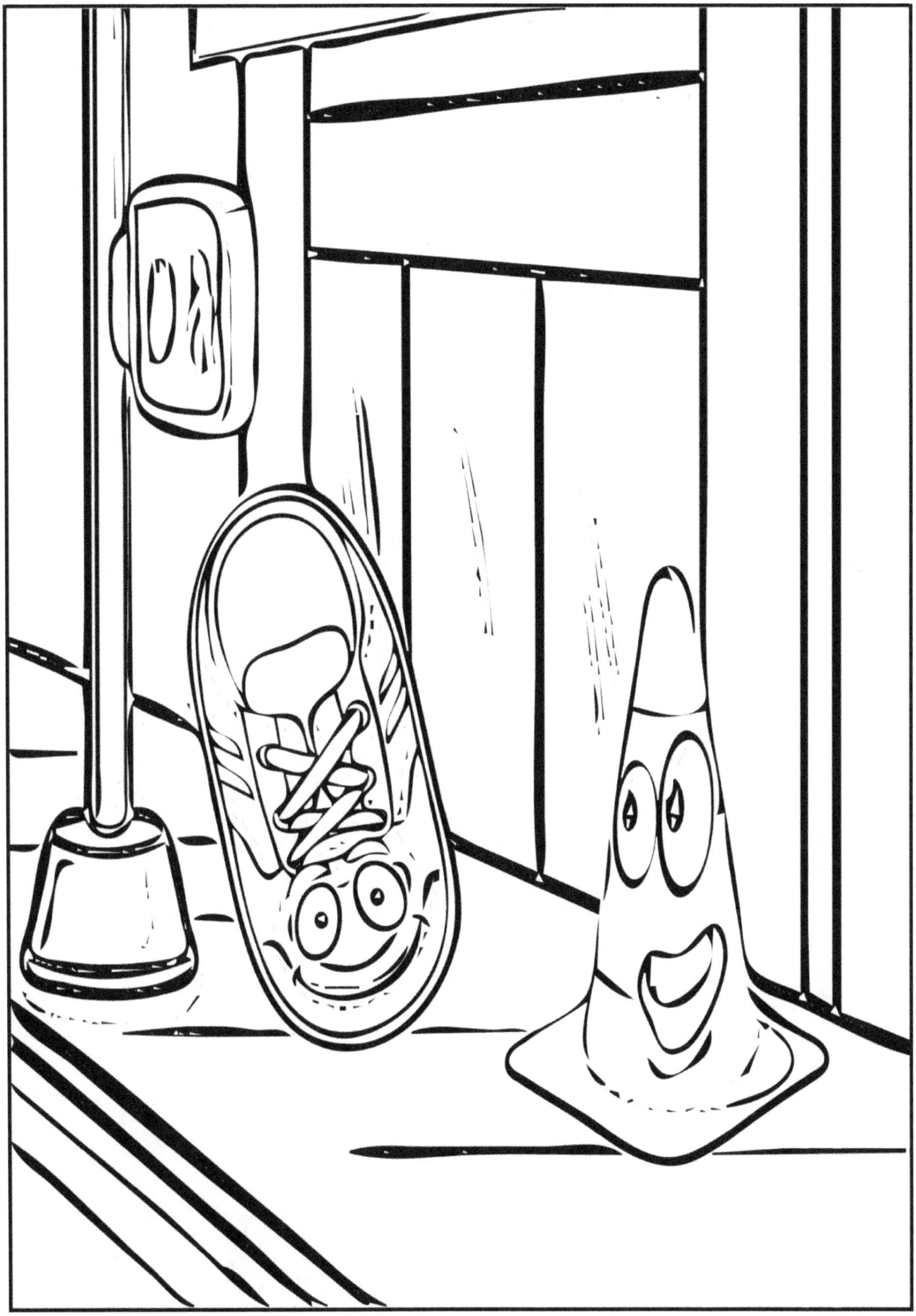

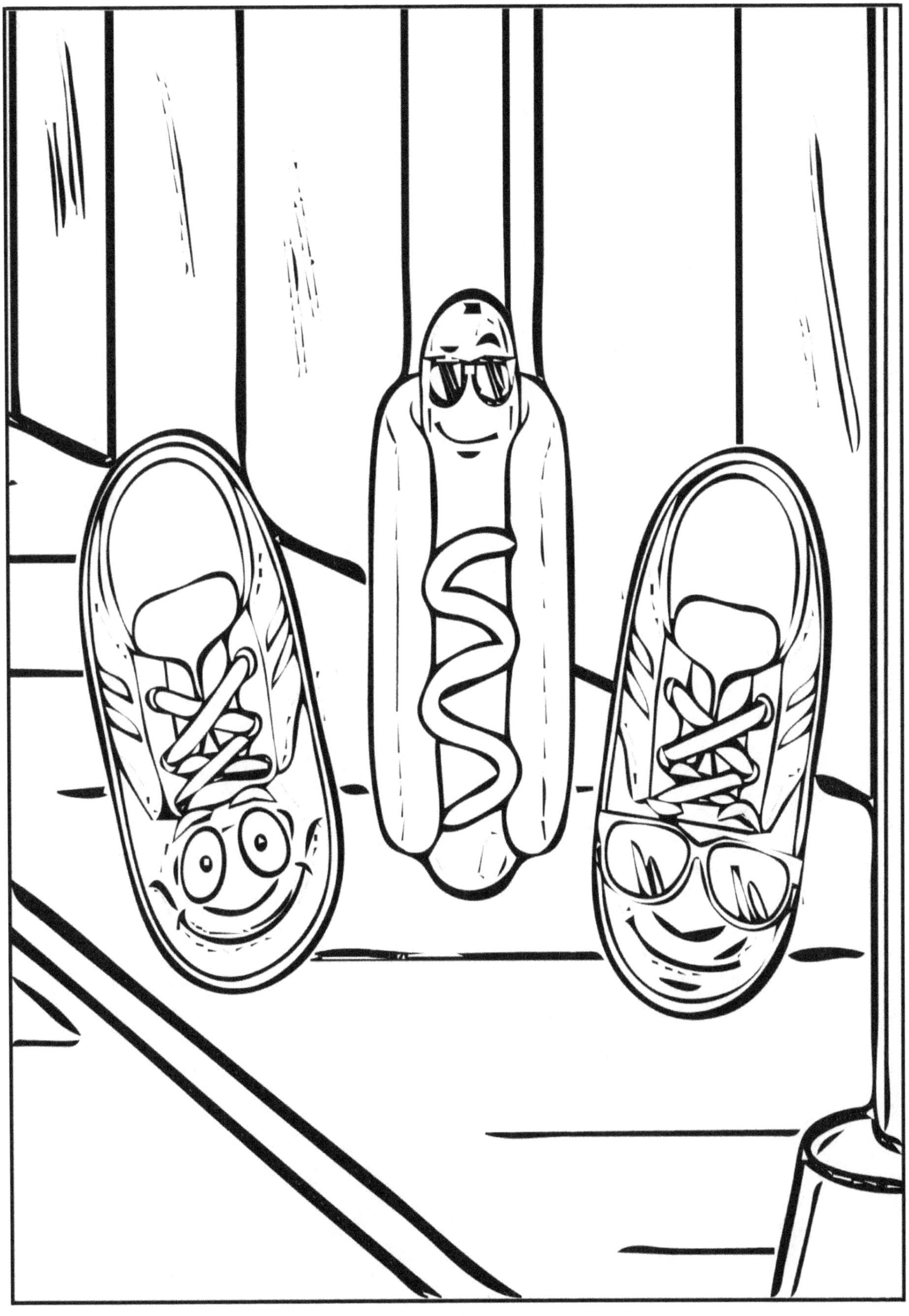

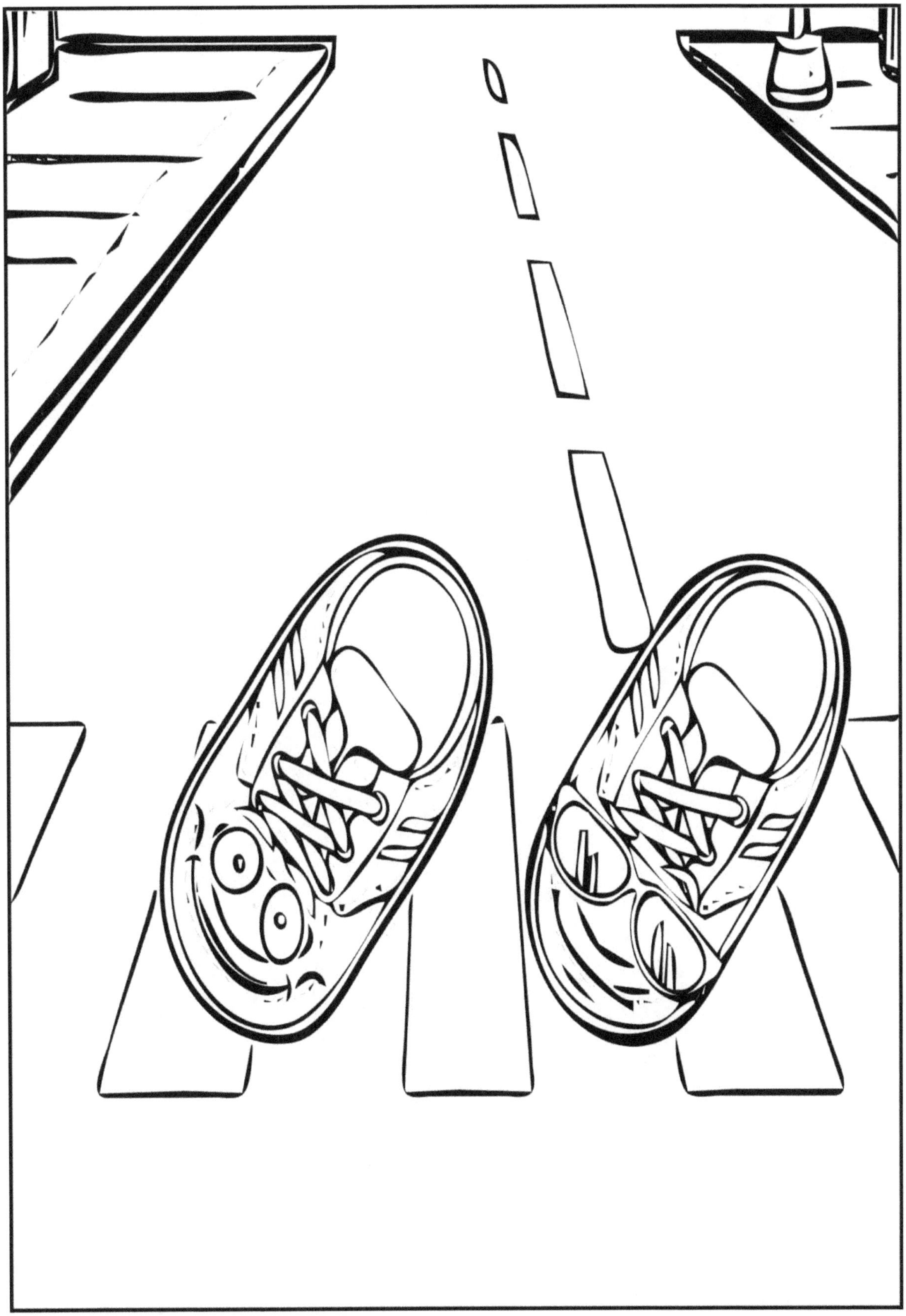

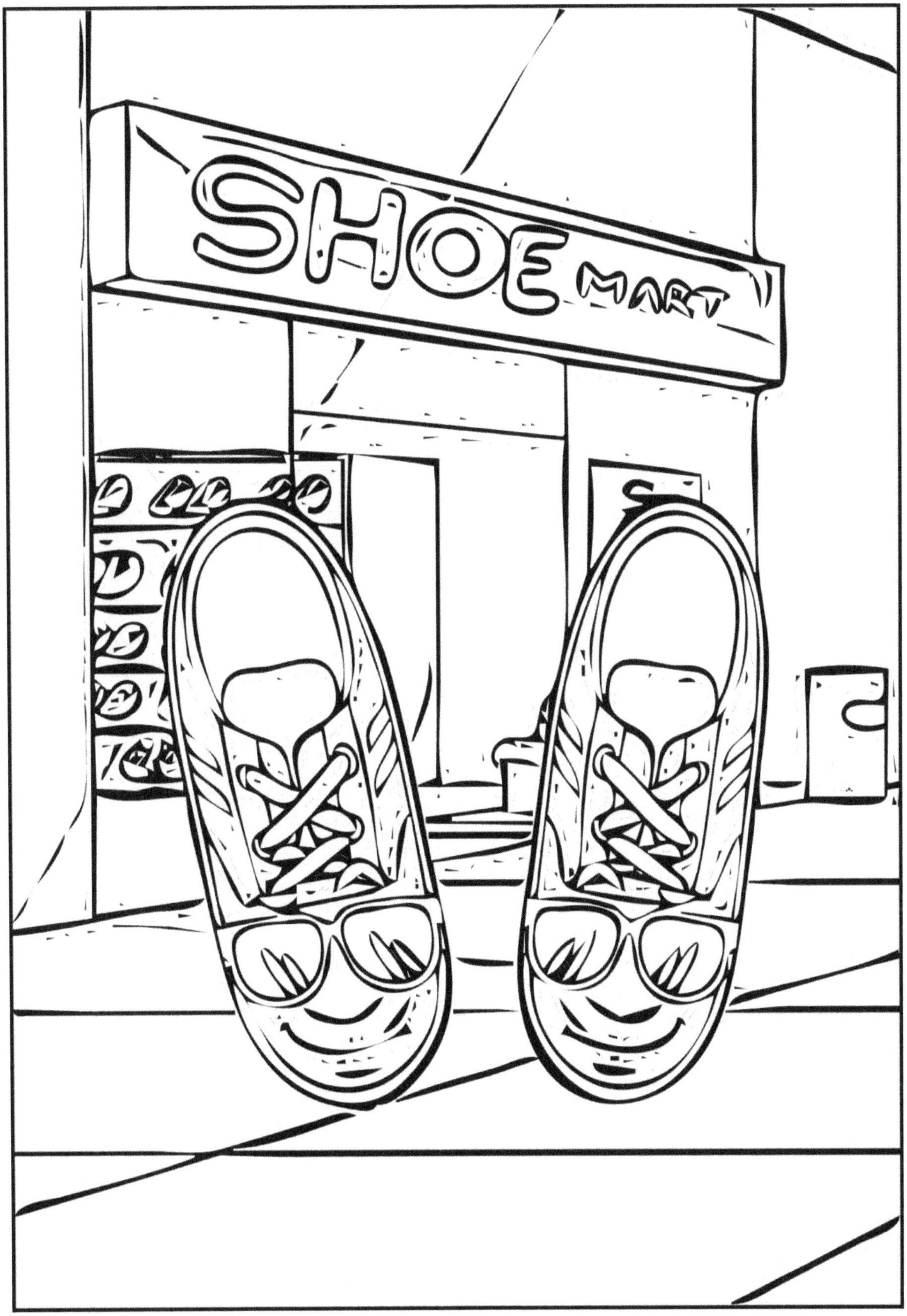
SHOE
MART

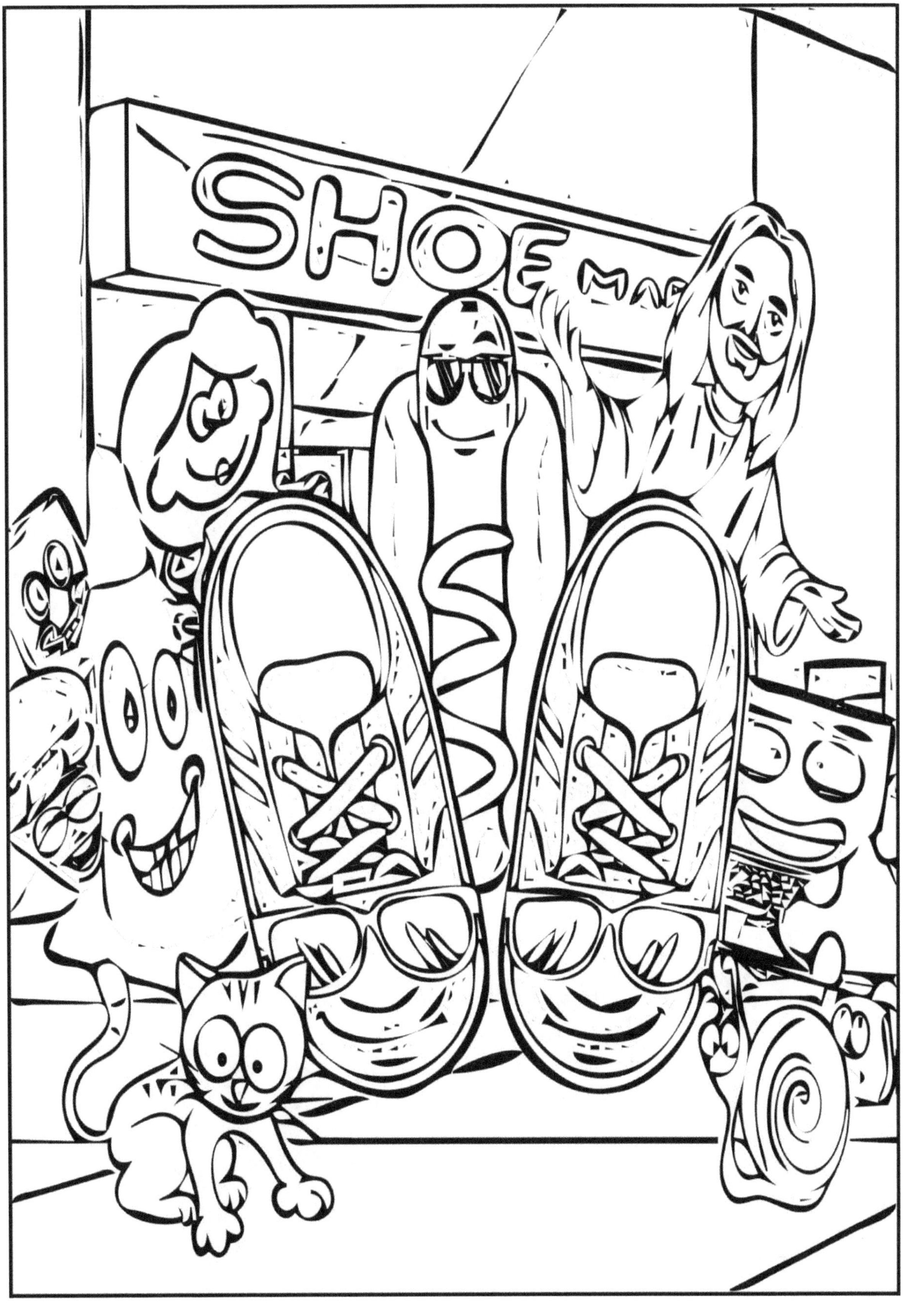
SHOE

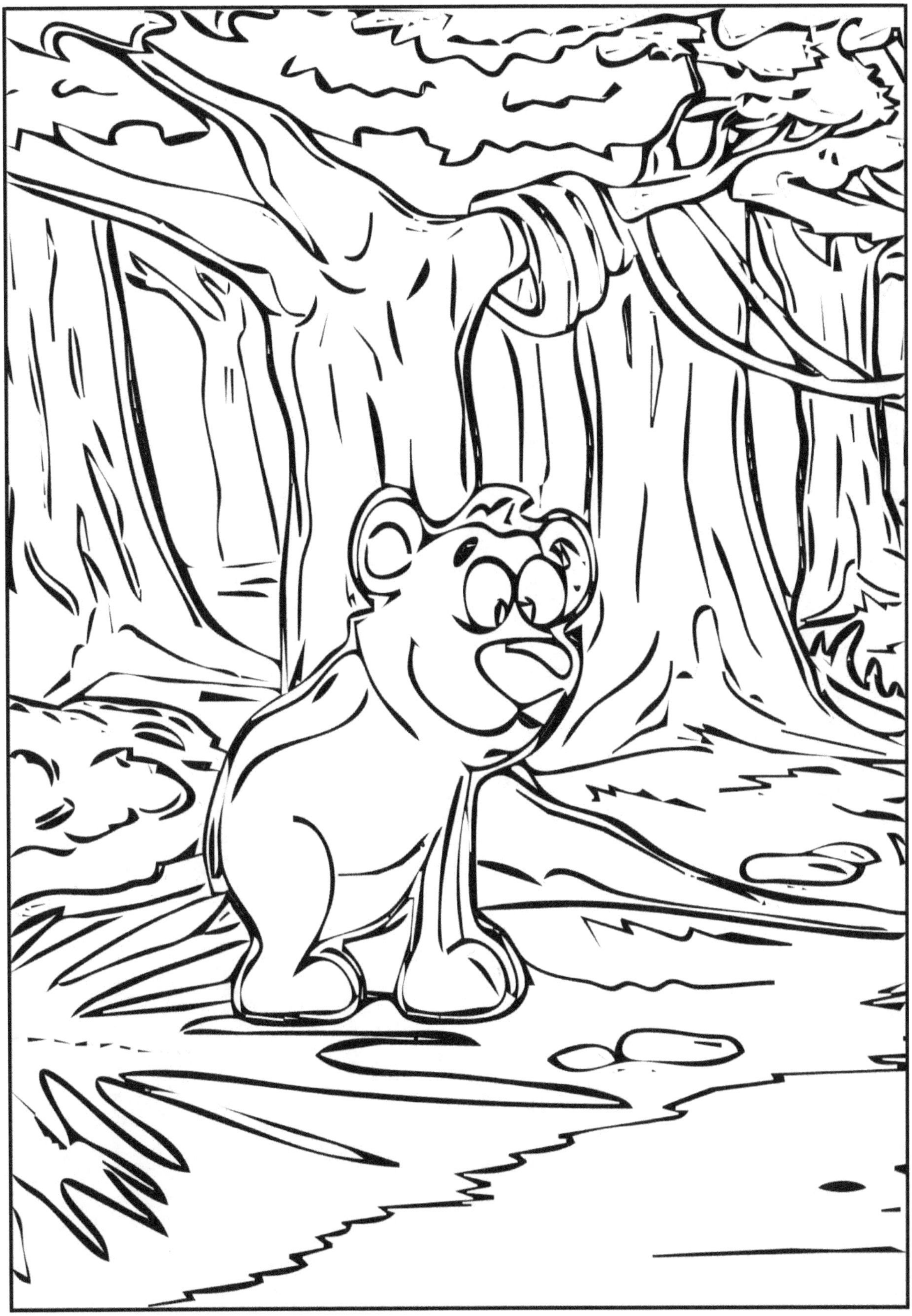

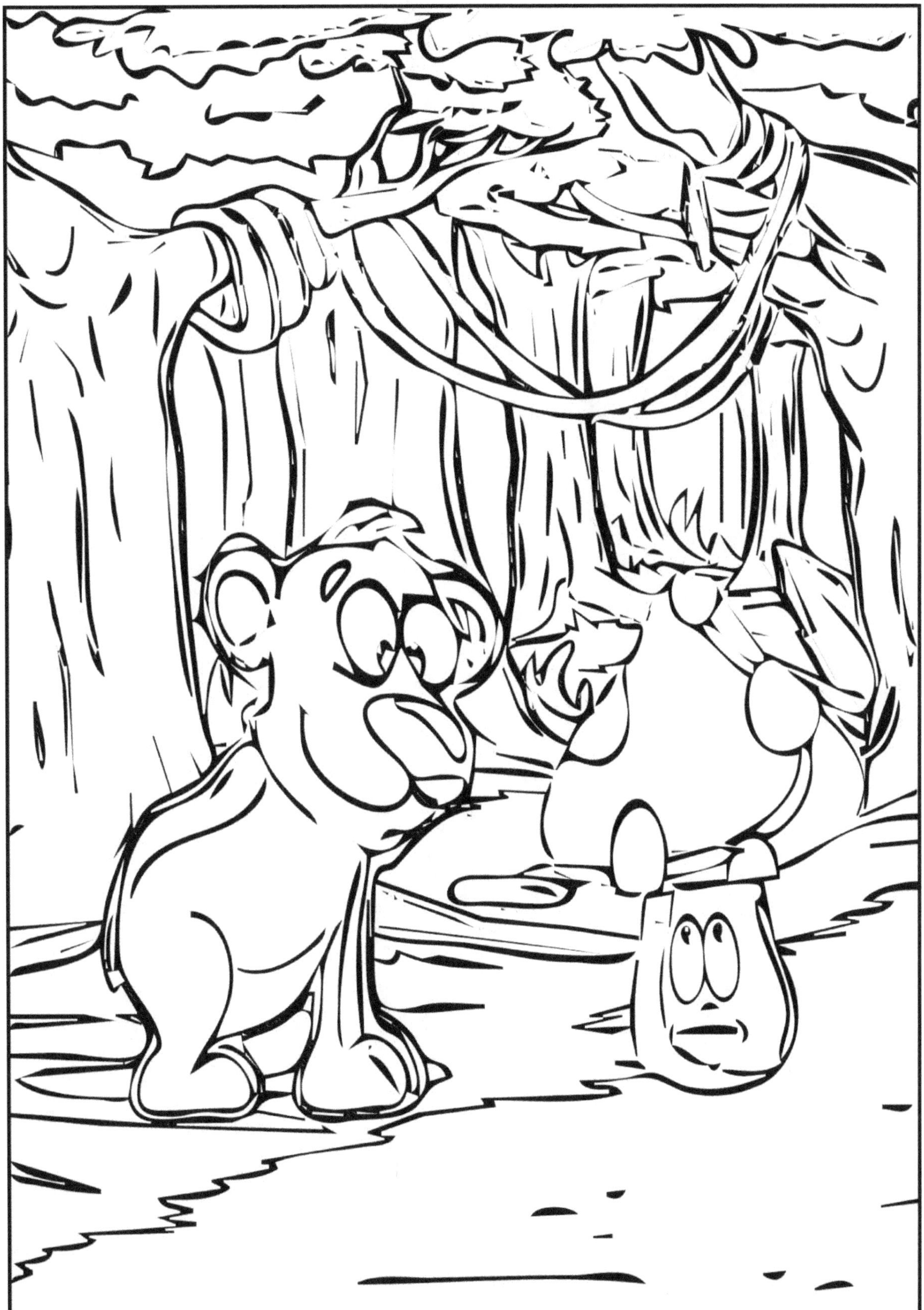

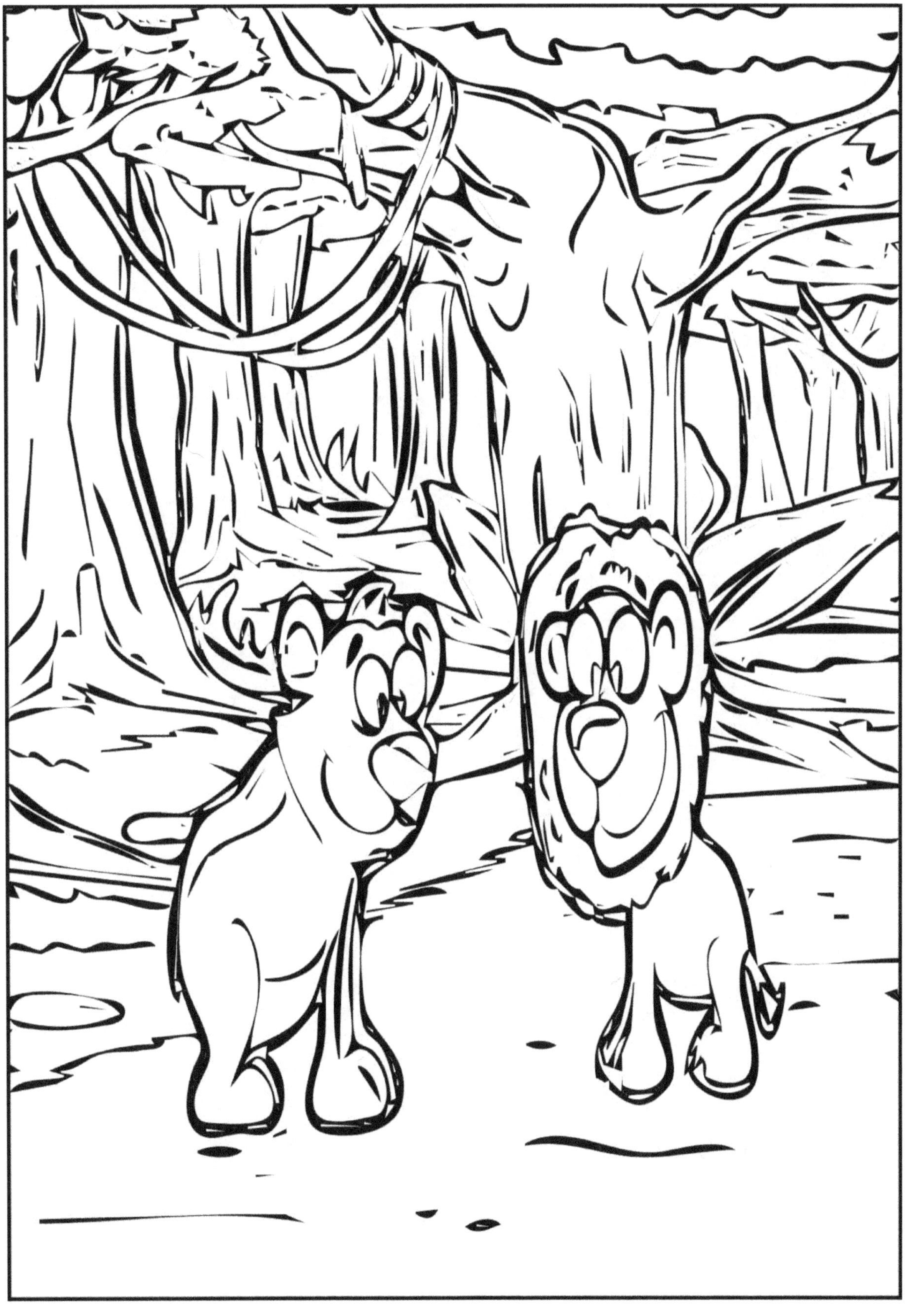

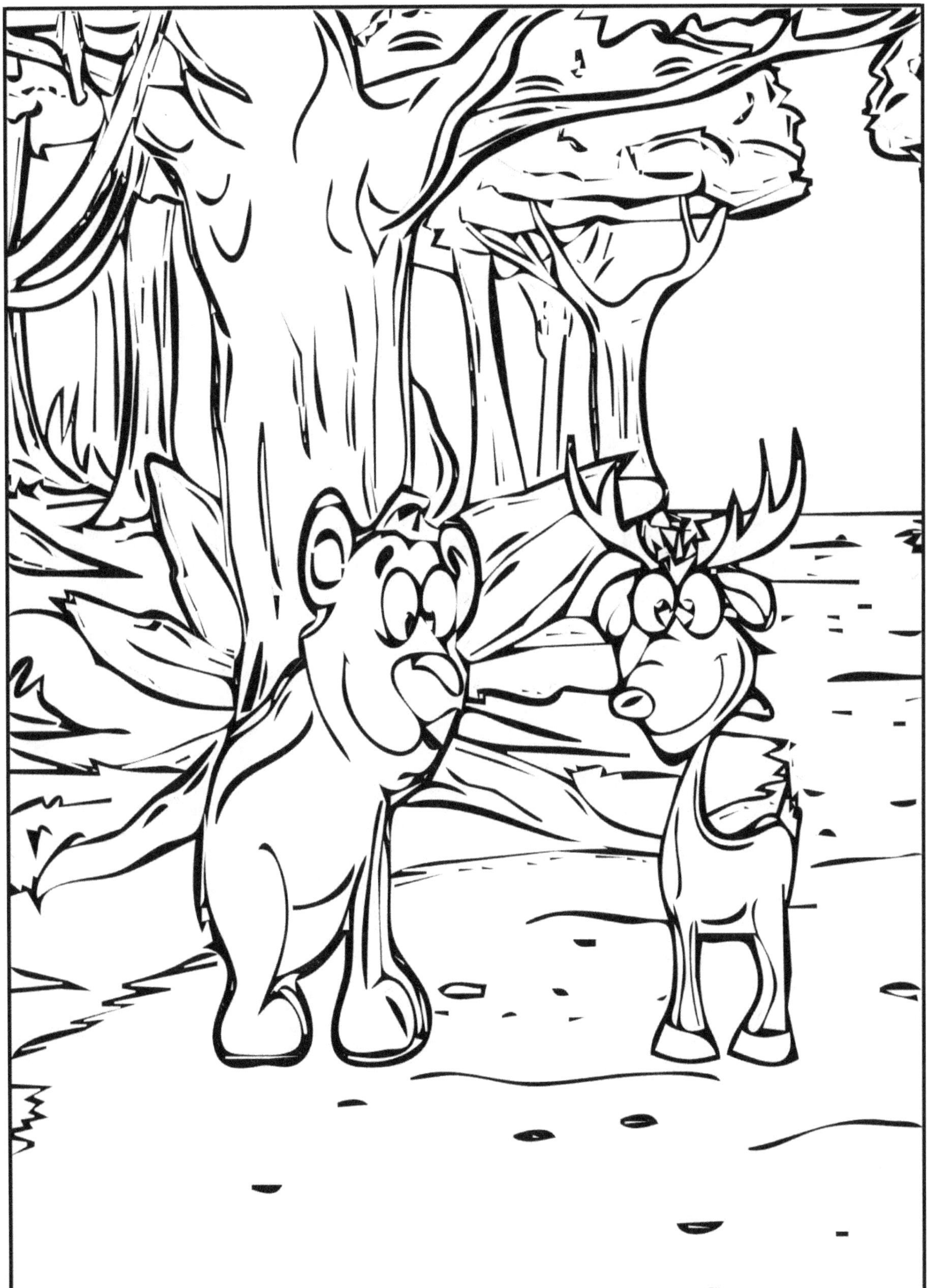

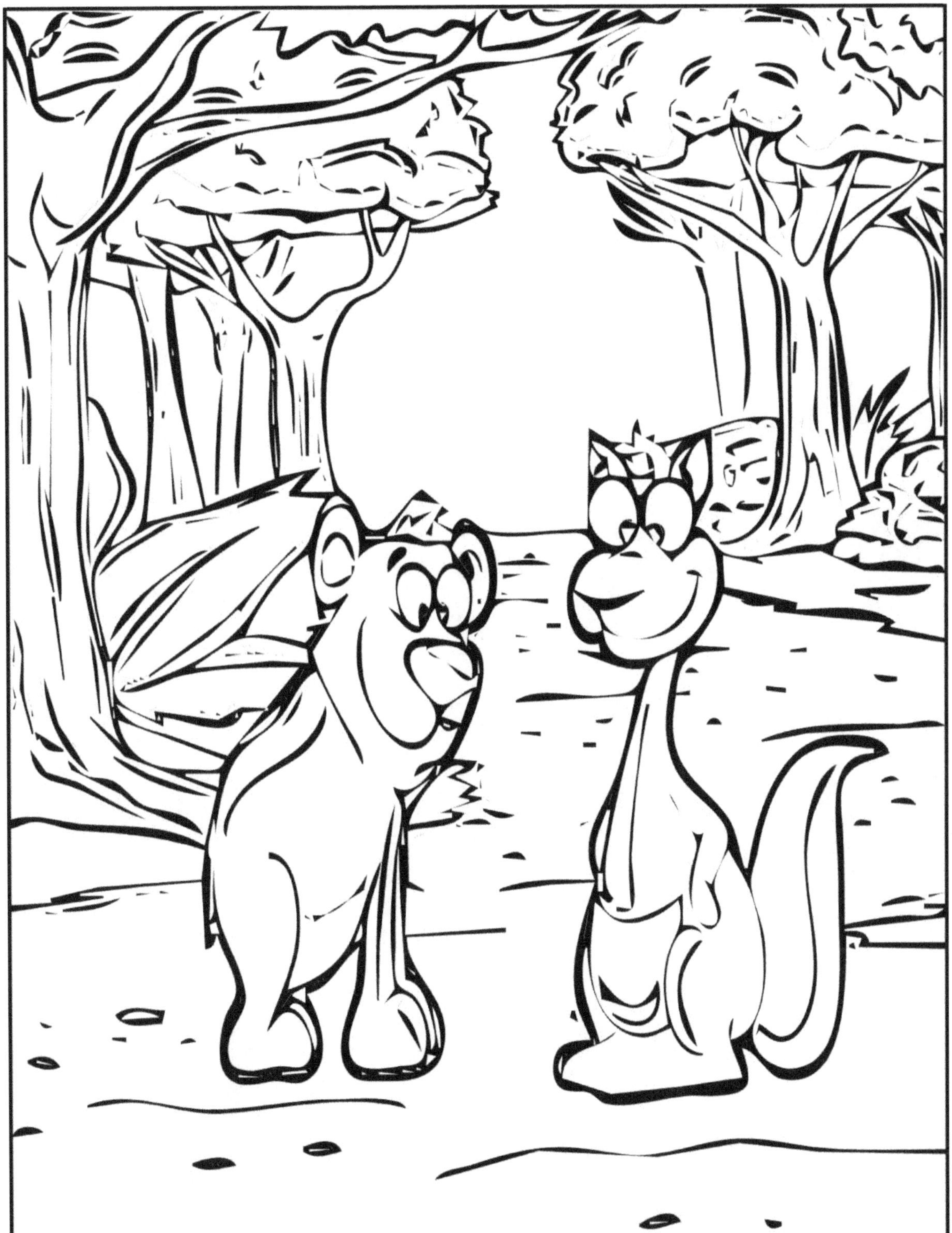

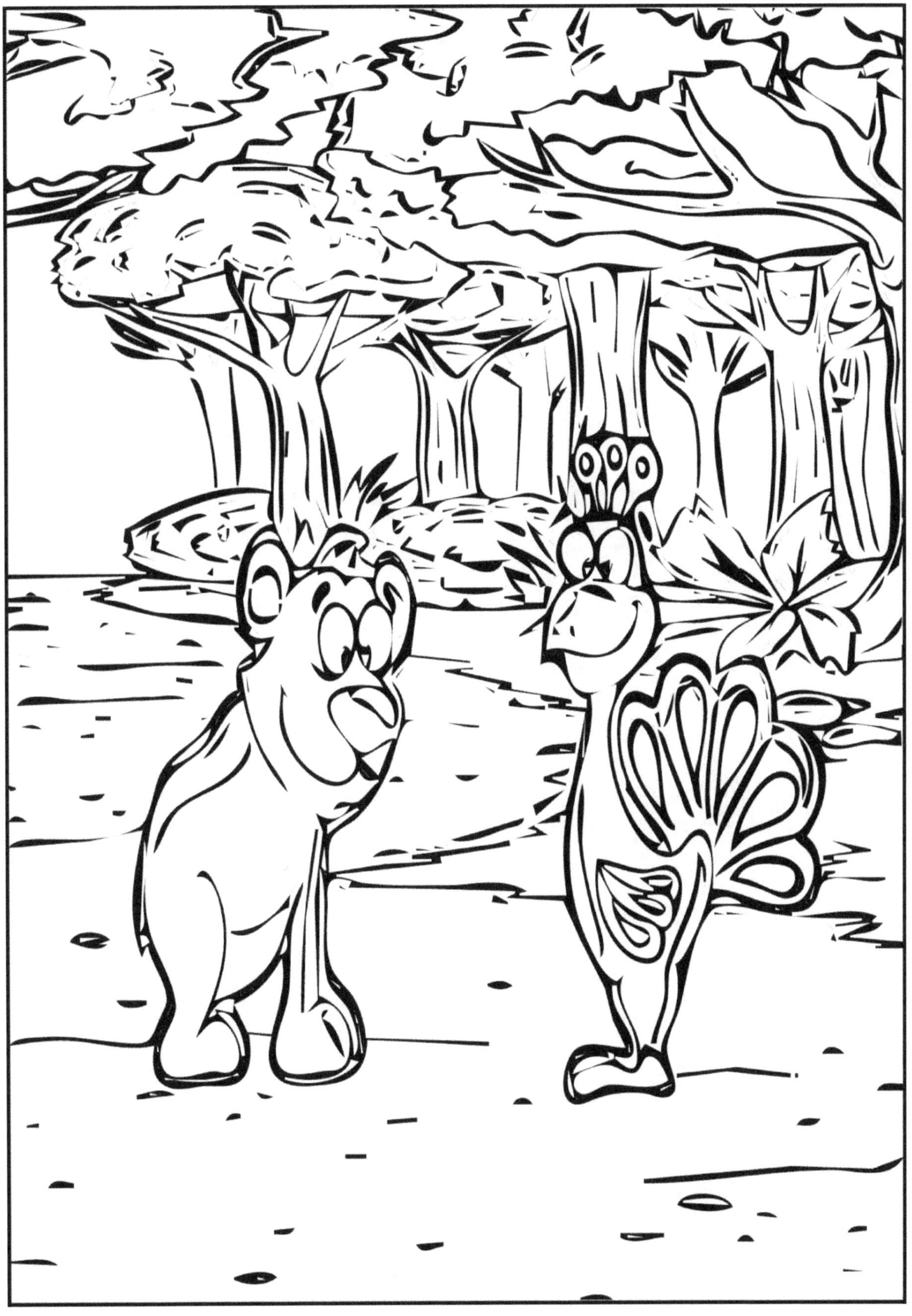

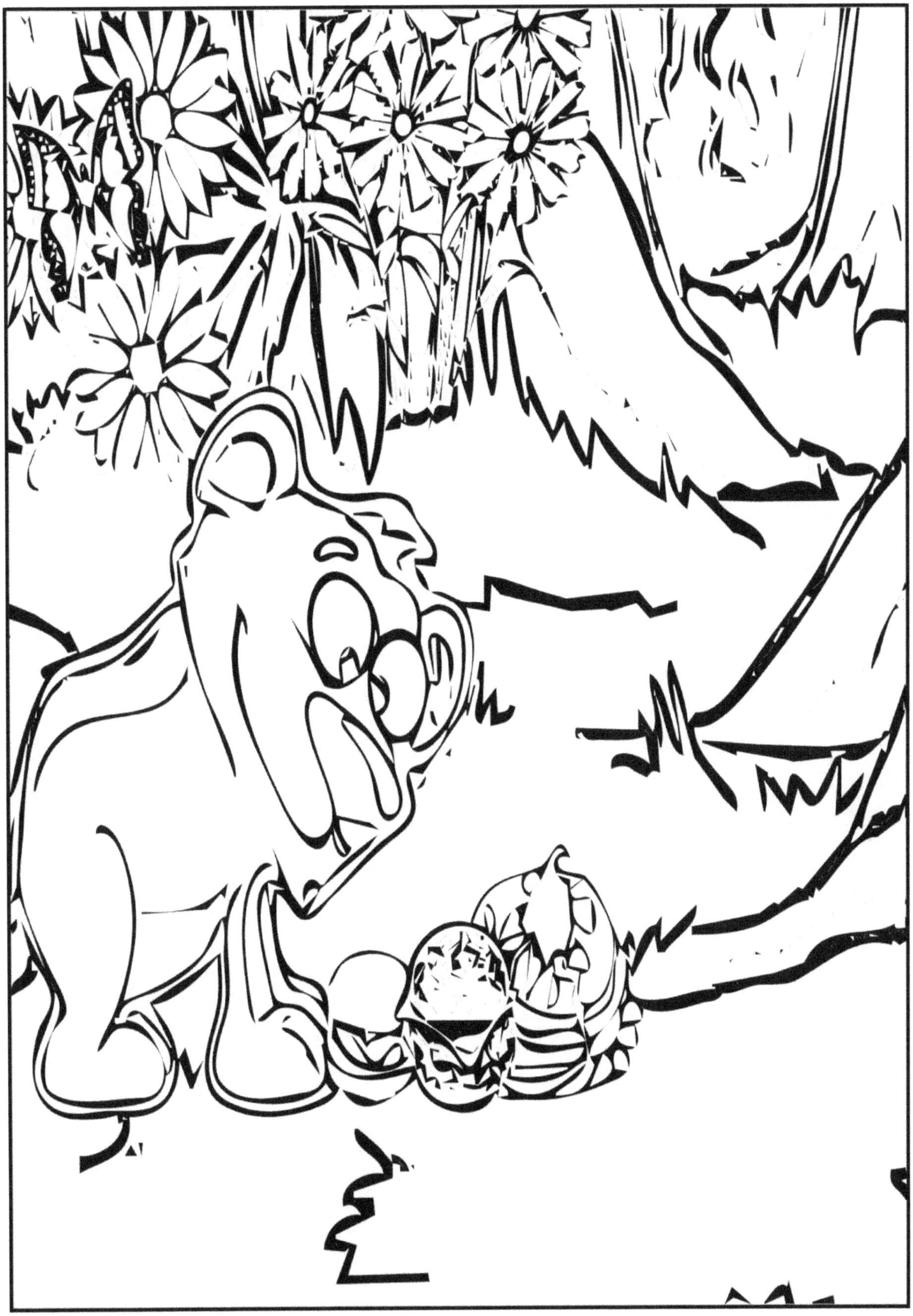

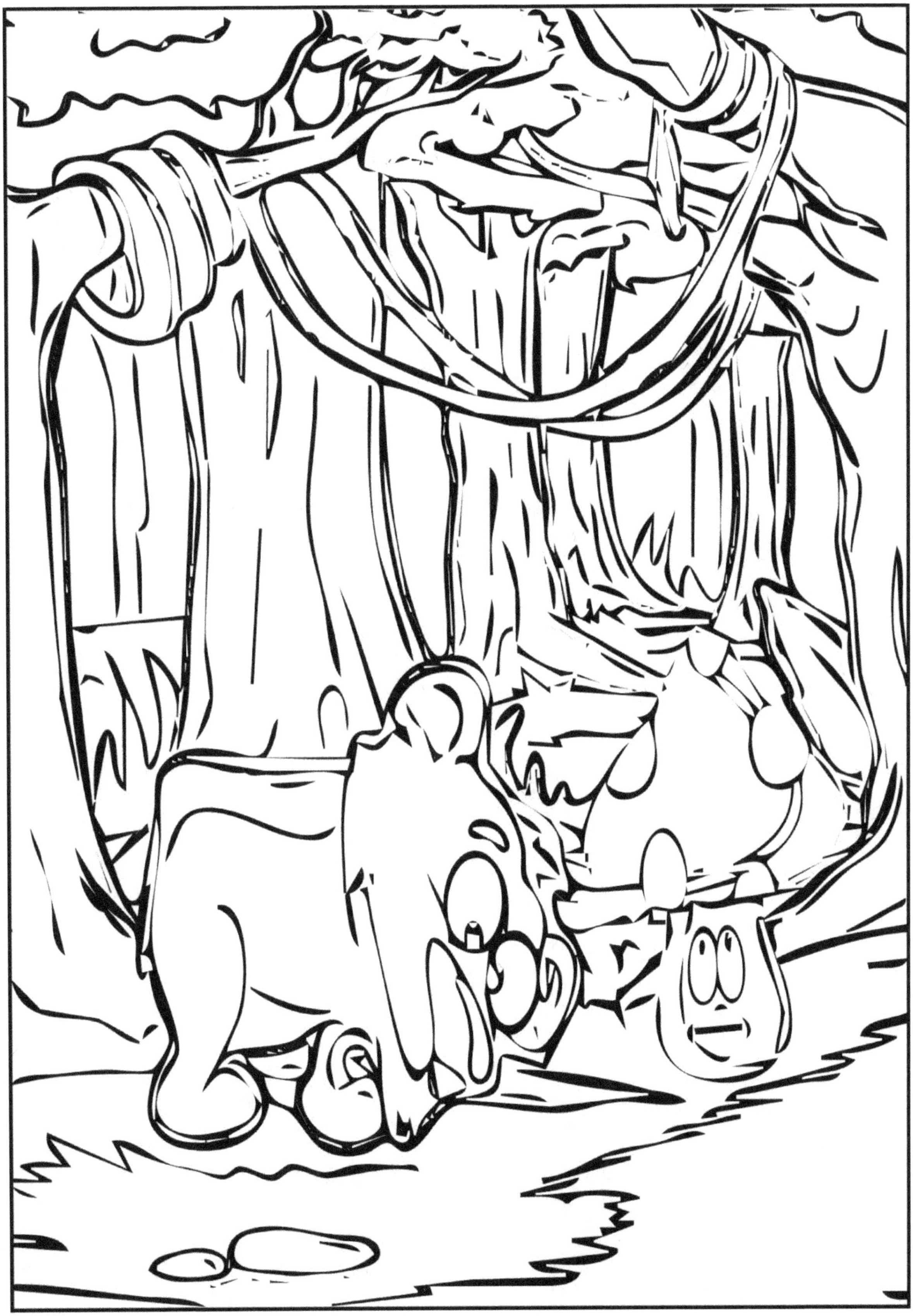

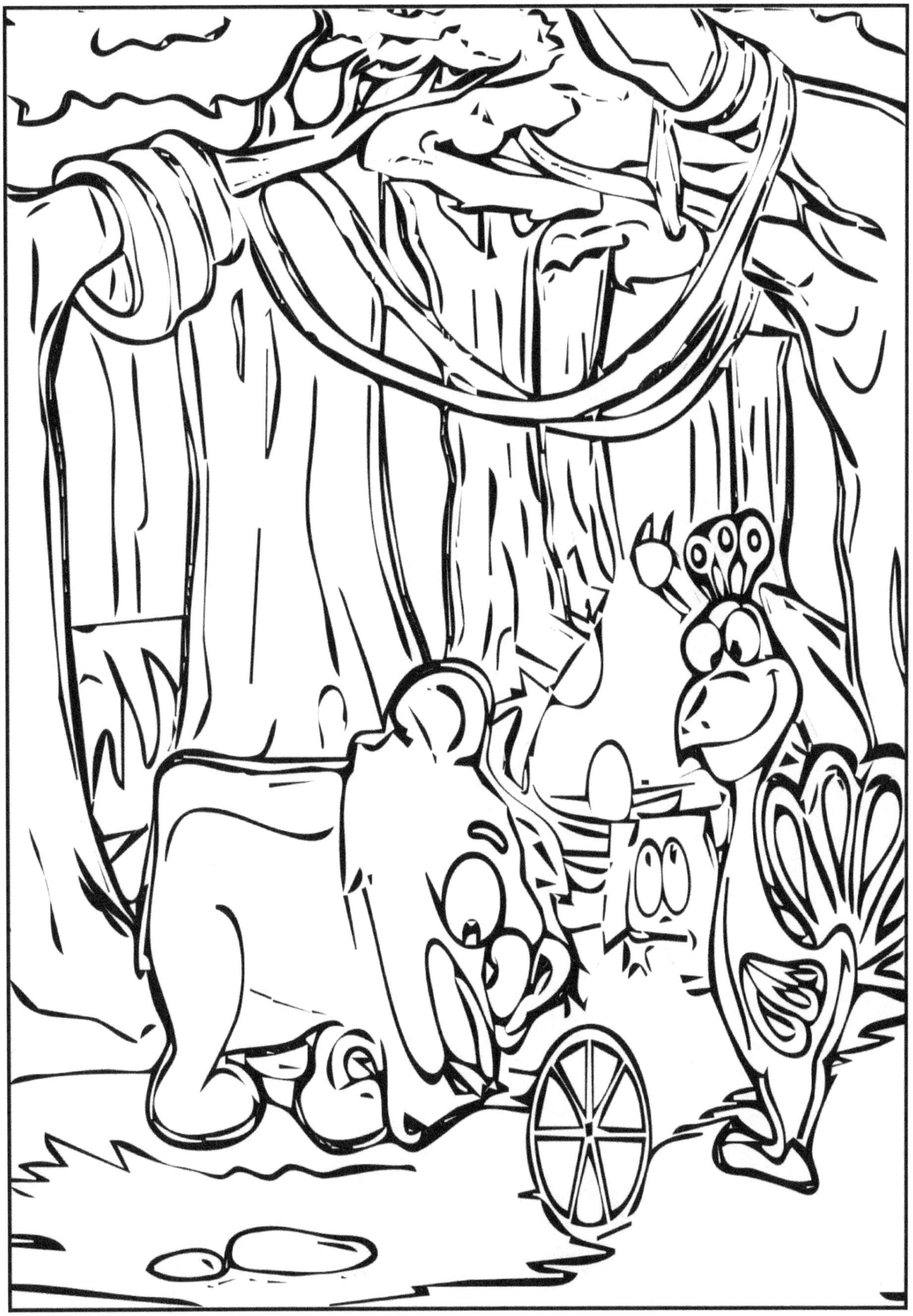

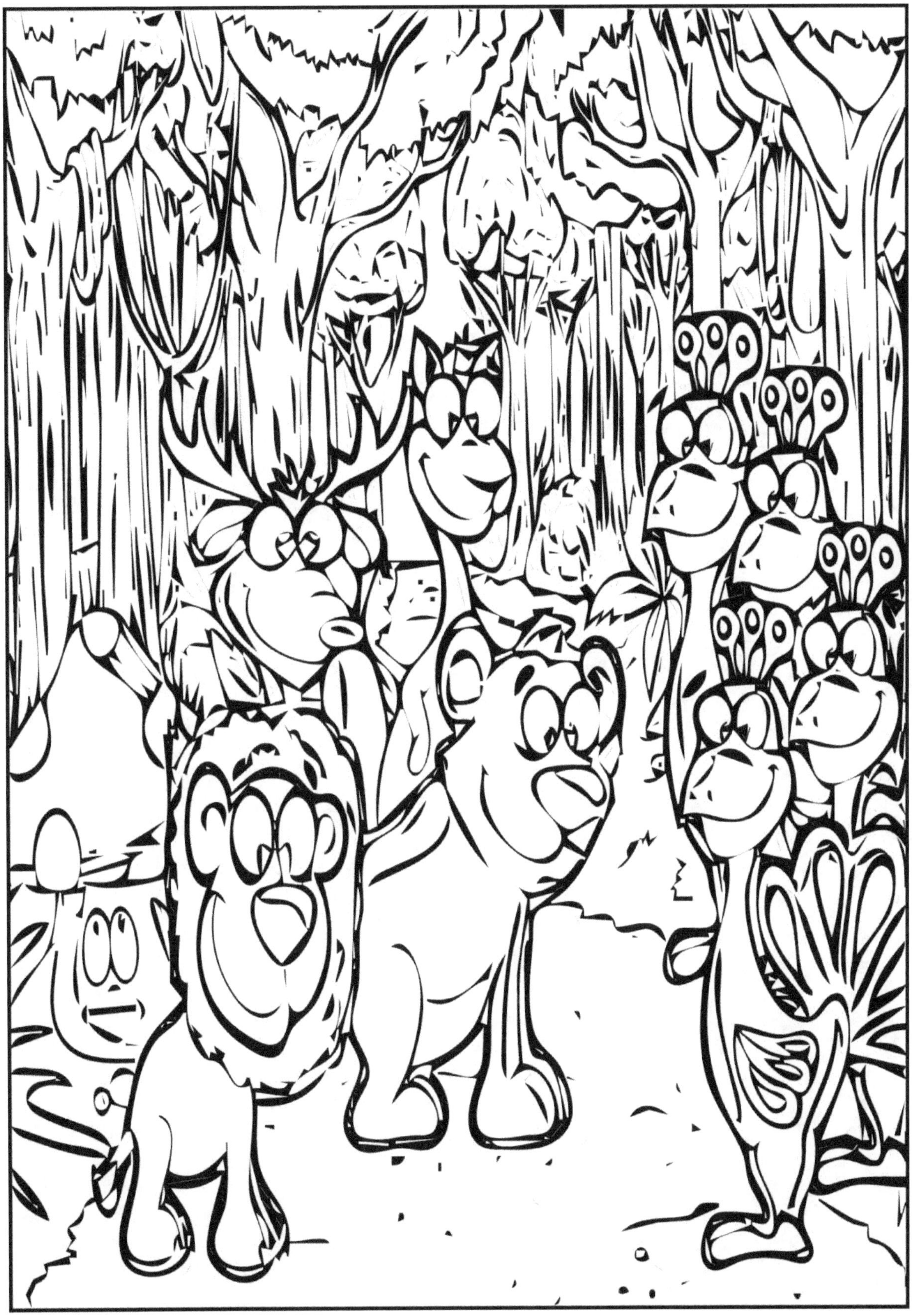

www.ingramcontent.com/pod-product-compliance
Lightning Source LLC
Chambersburg PA
CBHW080610180526
45168CB00007B/2861